CATechisms

poems
by

John Delaney

Finishing Line Press
Georgetown, Kentucky

CATechisms

To *Ramen, the Brahmin*

and all the other cats (and dogs) that enriched my life with sweetness, kindness, and love

Copyright © 2025 by John Delaney
ISBN 979-8-89990-188-1 First Edition
All rights reserved under International and Pan-American Copyright Conventions. No part of this book may be reproduced in any manner whatsoever without written permission from the publisher, except in the case of brief quotations embodied in critical articles and reviews.

Publisher: Leah Huete de Maines
Editor: Christen Kincaid
Cover art and photographs of Ramen: John Delaney
Author photo: Evelyn van Naerssen
Cover design: John Delaney

Order online: www.finishinglinepress.com
also available on amazon.com

Author inquiries and mail orders:
Finishing Line Press
PO Box 1626
Georgetown, Kentucky 40324
USA

Contents

Adopting a Cat: Checklist 1

Playing with the Cat 3

Tête-à-Tête 5

Reading with the Cat 7

Prelude (to a Nap), in C Major 9

Bubble Wrap 11

Eat, Play, Love—Sleep 13

Pacemaker 15

Cat Karaoke 17

Caveat 19

The Battle for the Box 21

Coat 23

Prepping for the Cat 25

The Stations 27

Breakfast Chez Chat 29

Morning Muse, or, A-musing 31

Scratching Post 33

Cat Hotel 35

Cosy Conceits 37

Ventriloquist 39

Wishful Watching 41

Prescription 43

Heartthrobs 45

When-You-Just-Want-to-Clear-Your-Head-Not-Think Yoga 47

Dream Buddies 49

Watching Cat TV 51

Inspector #1 53

Hair Day 55

Lost Sleep Found 57

Waiting 59

On the Porch 61

Pillow Talk 63

Ramen, the Brahmin 65

CATalogue 67

Cat at the Window 69

Acknowledgments 71

Author Biography / About This Book 73

"If man could be crossed with the cat, it would improve man, but it would deteriorate the cat." —Mark Twain

"There are two means of refuge from the miseries of life: music and cats." —Albert Schweitzer

"What greater gift than the love of a cat." —Charles Dickens

"Time spent with cats is never wasted." —Sigmund Freud

"Your house will always be blessed with love, laughter, and friendship if you have a cat." —Lewis Carroll

"A cat purring on your lap is more healing than any drug in the world, as the vibrations you are receiving are of pure love and contentment." —Saint Francis of Assisi

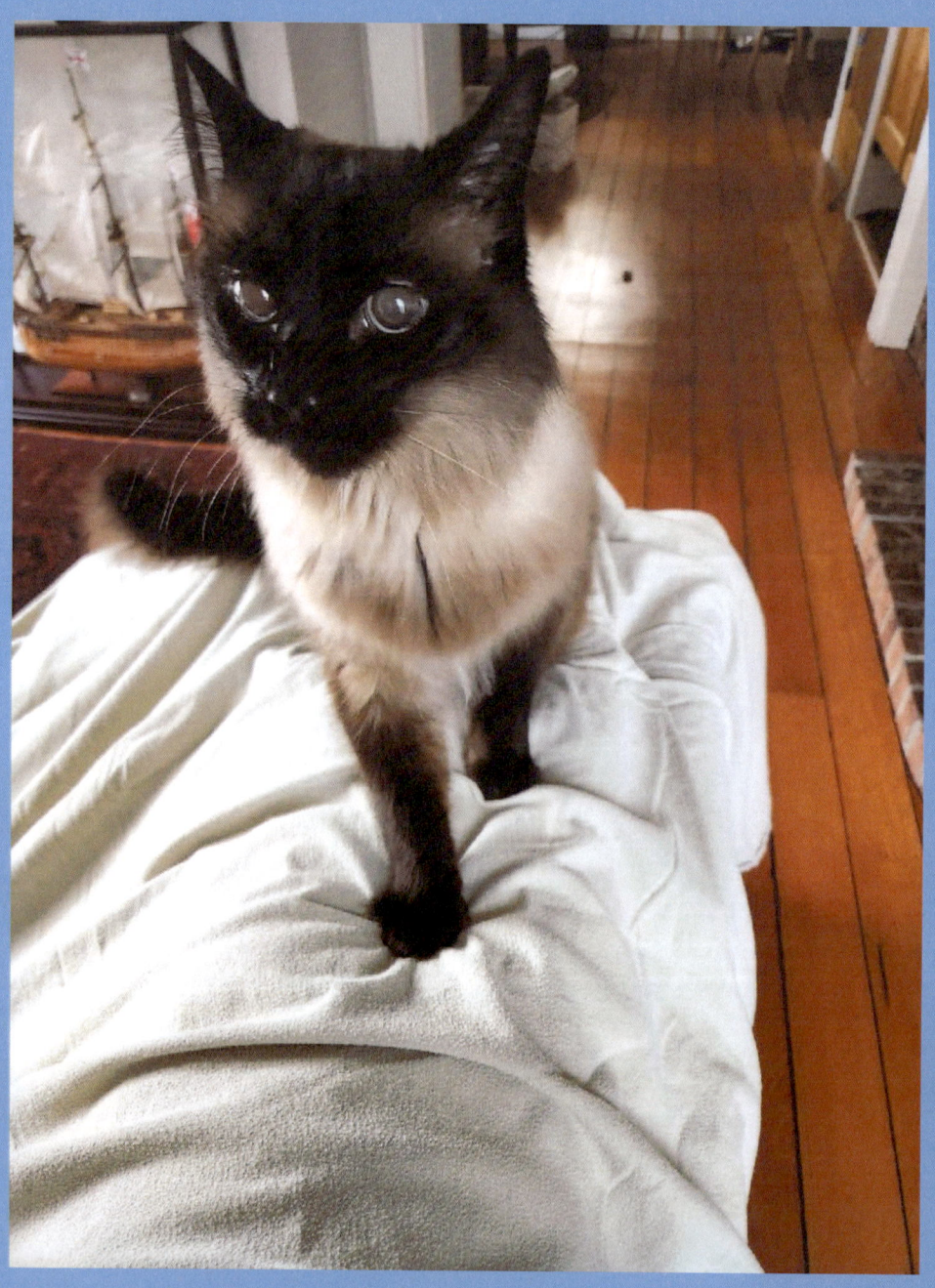

Adopting a Cat: Checklist

Taunts the long shadows with maudlin meows. √

Explores every nook and cranny. Canny. √

Finds hiding places in storage spaces. √

Resumes eating habits, with treating perks. √

Bears the litter box as daily detox. √

Toys with the joys of empty paper bags. √

Purrs pat approval of each petting pal. √

Sleeps to daydream and/or daydreams to sleep. √

Claws scratching post to exorcise his ghost. √

Curls a catnap around your tempting lap. √

Kneads on your chest his leavening dough. √

Gifts freely his love, offered a home of. √

Bless that kindness has found you and bound you.
Now tender your heart till death do you part. √√

Playing with the Cat

He pretends not to take interest
in the string of yarn snaking by,
but snags it sharply with his paw
just when it heads undercover.

I'm 72, sitting on the floor
with an old cat. We might as well
be buddies at a bar: one blabberer,
one seemingly absorbed in his thoughts,
tasked for an occasional opinion.

What are we doing here in the white light
of eternity, stabbing at yarn and words,
occupied by their entertainment?
There's really no point to this, Kitty,
except that we enjoy it together.

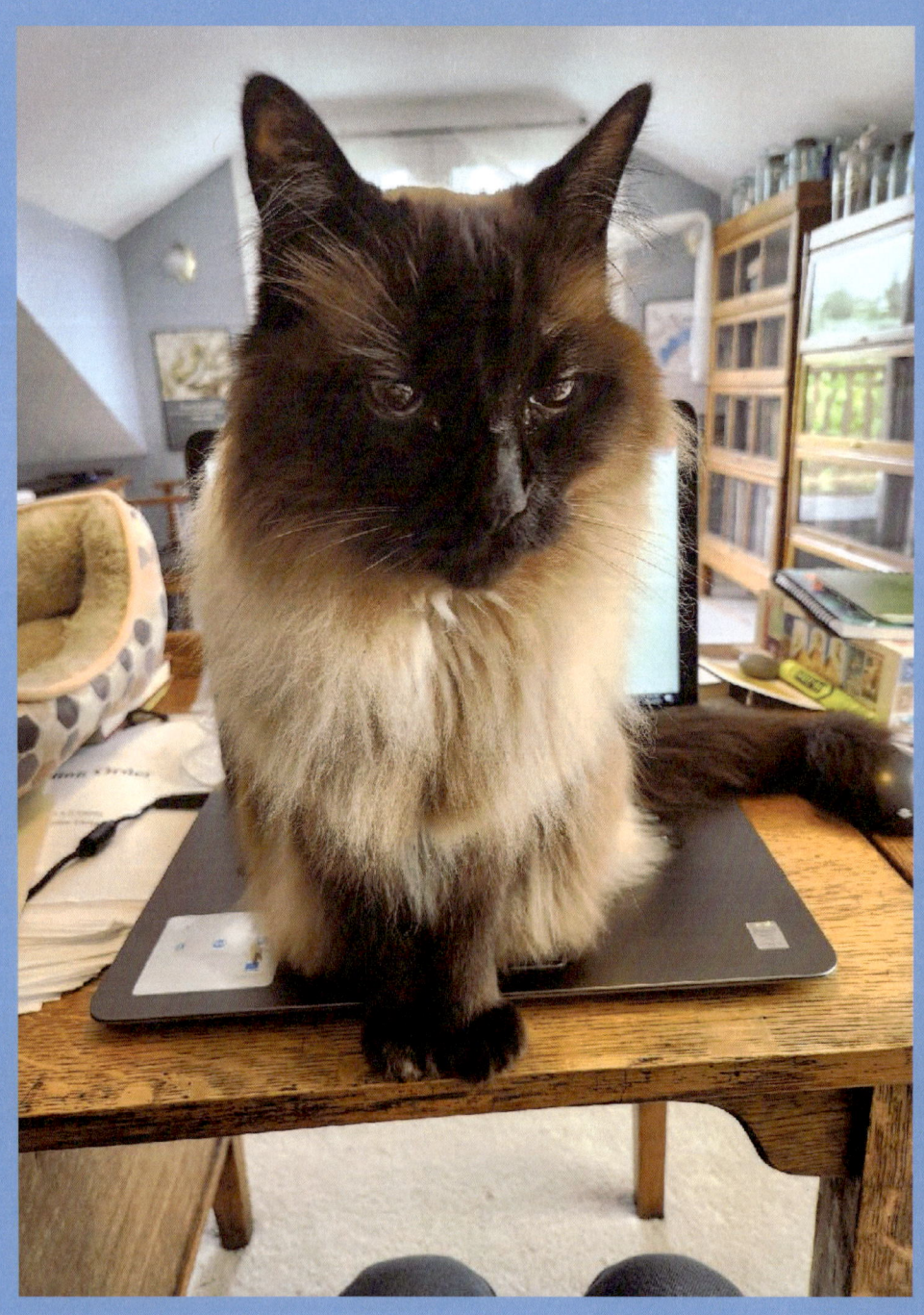

Tête-à-Tête

He jumps onto the desk and steps over
to the laptop as if on a mission,
sitting down on the keyboard, facing me.
His eyes glisten and his Persian mane roars.
My work has begun to move off the screen
due to the keys his body keeps pressing.
I bring my forehead forward, touching his,
and then he rubs his head hard against mine,
nuzzling the hair and even licking it.
Then something extraordinary happens,
I think, between the meeting of our minds.
While we hold our heads together there,
kicklines of z's advance up the blank page
of the screen like dancing theta brain waves.

Reading with the Cat

I'm reading a book about snails
with the weight of my cat on my lap.
As the warmth of his body spreads,
I warm up to the cold-blooded topics
of slime and whorls and tentacled eyes.
I become a conduit for their worlds,
the cat curled up in his furry dreams,
the snail on a slime-enabled journey.

But then the cat lifts his head out of sleep,
giving his backside a few quick licks,
and stares cold into the feckless room,
as if he, too, had slid out of a shell
on a whim to see what the prospects were,
yet, instead of heading out, heads back in.

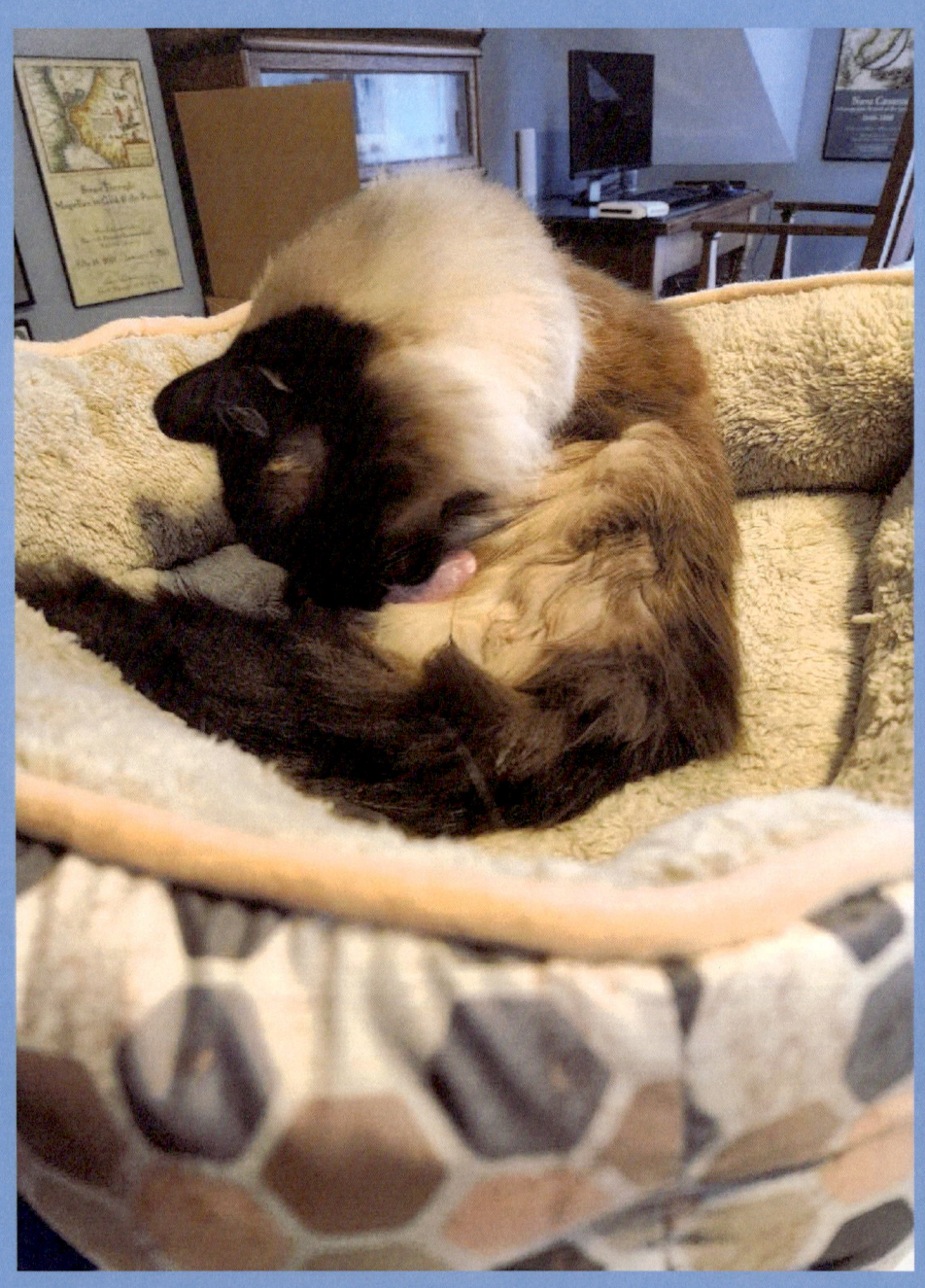

Prelude (to a Nap), in C Major
Apologies to Johann Sebastian Bach

After a meal, your good manners require
a cleanup as a prelude to a nap.

Meticulously, you wash your body
with long laps of your tongue, even your paws
which then wet-wipe that whiskered, wizened face,
those tufted ears. Tongue lickings and lashings,
and lavishings, until it's time to curl
that contrapuntal tail around a theme
and bury your head deep into its fugue.

From all appearances, it would seem
you're composing a prelude to a dream.

Bubble Wrap

He jumps into the open cardboard box
onto bubble wrapping at the bottom.
How well the medium inspires play!
The crinkly cracking sounds, the scrunching up.
Hiding under wraps and sudden popping.
Or just sitting there, luxuriating
within the confines of cat imagination.

He shames me to find joy in little things.
His walnut brain more curious than mine,
less willing to take everything for granted,
challenged to coax objects back to life
with the prodding of his paw's forgiving.
I'll never gripe I'm bored to death again.

Nor dare say that life is not worth living.

Eat, Play, Love—Sleep
      Apologies to Elizabeth Gilbert (author, Eat, Pray, Love*)*

It's the routine you develop
to keep you comfortable in this life,
healthy and, may I say, even safe.

My cat is very happy in his
and makes no effort to hide it:
eat, play and love, with lots of sleep.

He's flexible in the order,
except for eating, which must come first,
for which he prepares well in advance

by meddling in the kitchen,
meowing to make his wishes known.
Play can happen at any time

an object strikes his fancy
and draws an investigation
with the probing of a paw.

At least twice a day he seeks out
petting on my lap, purring
his level of satisfaction.

He uses sleep as intermission
or cushion between the rest.
Eating is tiring and so is play.

Loving is a way that leads to sleep,
which we never get enough of.
Work, of course, is part of our routine,

necessary in the broader picture.
But Kitty rather doubts it.
He gets nine lives without it.

Pacemaker

When my heart rate hovered in the forties,
I had a pacemaker inserted.
It gave me a minimum of sixty.
When I walk up a hill now, I don't faint
or feel dizzy: oxygen deserted.
Each second I can count as a heartbeat.

The cat on my chest was a backup plan,
purring from a different kind of motor
that reliably lifted my spirits up.
That sparkling flame held in his eyes there,
truly one of life's wonders to behold—
why I locked my hands round the loaf
of his body in the form of prayer,
grateful for him, my beating heart controlled.

Cat Karaoke

My cat will do anything to get me up.
His wake-up calls start rolling down the hall,
and reach a crescendo outside my door,
which is open, by the way. There he sits,
waiting for the effect. Not getting any—
rather, not getting what he expected,
I'm telling him to 'shush' and go away—
he jumps up on the bed to argue closer,
getting on top of my chest or my side
and looking deeply (I guess) in the dark
at my imponderable form of resistance.
So he resorts to the soft touch of a paw
while beginning to purr his persuasion
in karaoke. That works. Okey-dokey.

Caveat

Hail him knight, not knave,

my caveman in his man cave!

Enclave of the brave.

Unless it's under the blanket you crave!

The Battle for the Box

Was over on the first day,
with the cat sitting in it, gloating.
He had chewed through its defense
and rendered its ramparts
all over the battlefield.

On succeeding days, he'd return
to bolster his glory,
further shredding the walls,
lowering their resistance,
strewing its residue.

Neither pacifier nor unifier,
he proved to be an occupier.

Coat

When you were sleeping on my lap,
I closely examined your coat,
the hairs so soft and fine yet dense,
colored like a woman's ombré,
subtly drawn out from brown to white.

There you were, so deep in your nap,
as my fingers so gently wrote
their love across your body. Hence-
forth, you'll wear another coat, I pray,
from day to night, from dark to light.

Prepping for the Cat

Being your human being, I tell him,
especially early in the morning
when he climbs on my chest at 5 A.M.,
requires ritual preparation.
'Bud, I need to pee and take a shower.'
We have to wait for the water to warm,
whether to shampoo or follow my norm.

Outside the glass, he questions my antics,
when afterwards I wipe the walls down
and he paws at the squeegee's sweeping moves.
When I step out, of course he thinks I'm done,
rubbing against the towel as I dry.
I stand before the mirror, pull out the drawer,
take my pills, put my eyedrops in. 'POOR, POOR,

KITTY, there's more.' Donning deodorant,
lotion, combing my hair. Sometimes I shave,
though it's not a necessity with beards.
Then what to wear? What's the weather doing?
'You're so lucky to be dressed and ready
to go. If only you could tell *me-how*.'
He does, of course, and often. That's him now.

The Stations

To and from patrols to the litter box
and feeding bowl, he yowls his reports:
'all clear'. Then, like clockwork, mans the stations:
my chest in bed, my lap on couch or chair,
in his bed beside the laptop in the office.
Those are regular, self-imposed assignments.
But in my absence, there's another post
he's partial to partake: a sunny window roast.

Off duty, he makes exploratory
expeditions around the house, forays
into nooks and crannies, sniffing out
the enemy or finding friendly forces.
He target practices a mouse that jerks
erratically, strung along on a string,
and constantly cleans his dress uniform of fur.
Now he sits before me at attention:
                              'At your service, Sir.'

Breakfast *Chez Chat*

He thinks I've forgotten where the kitchen is,
urgently leading me there by the flag
of his upraised tail. I'm his sous-chef,
listening for more nuanced instructions
as he stretches his paws up to the counter.
I show him the can of salmon patė
I have chosen; like a good wine he sniffs
and approves. I mash half of it on the plate,
then take a small handful of hard pellets
of herring to embed in the paste
and drizzle some water over. After all,
I'm running a five-star cat restaurant.
Presentation is everything. I don
my maître d' role and offer the meal
on a saucer to prevent whisker fatigue.
Standing back, I wait for *le mot juste*: meow.

                  Can I go back to bed now?

Morning Muse, or, A-musing

Weighty and warm,
Kitty wedges himself in,
pinning my left arm down.
My right hand chicken-pecks
at the keyboard
and protects the mouse.

It's early, still dark;
the sun hasn't risen.
He purrs through his nose,
while I try to listen
to any new thoughts

rising on the rhythm
of my breathing.
Something will come to mind,
surely, about him,

his sleepyhead affection.
To snooze or muse,
that is the question.

Though he's decided,
I'm getting excited

to yawn at the dawn.

Scratching Post

Pretend it's tree bark
or something alive to dig into.
Claw and scratch,

Kitty. Leave your mark
on me, on my bleeding heart, natch.
Ooh!

Photographs by Theresa Berrett

Cat Hotel

'Don't be a tourist; be a traveler'—
great advice from my foreign country guide.
 Challenge yourself out of your comfort zone.
Taste the food that fuels its culinary art.
Amble down the wayward path; cross that bridge.
 Be confident if you're going alone.

Well, I might have modeled my cat instead.
There he was, right out of the box, testing
the waters, learning the ropes, seeking new heights,
practicing his skills on the environment.
And finding a comfortable spot to snooze
when he was tired of seeing the sights.

I don't have to worry, for I think it's true:
when I'm on vacation, my cat is too.

Cosy Conceits

'Snug as a bug' they would say,
when they had seen how my cat
outlines the opening
of this cushioned cave near the stove.

'The life of Riley' they would say,
after having seen how my kitty's
slumber sloop luxuriates
in this tropical, tranquil cove.

'Winner takes all' they'd say,
admiring the uncanny way
my buccaneer buddy
covertly covets this treasure trove.

Warmth is the magnet attracting
these iron-ic feline fetishes.

Ventriloquist

My cat has many voices.
Caterwauling early in the morning
in an attempt to awaken the world.
Directed meows at dinnertime
so he's not to be forgotten.
Much motor purring on my lap
or beside me, sometimes deeply drawn,
resonating up his throat through his nose.
A gentle, single mew when looking up
dreamily from a sleepy, comfy pose.

In his private world, though, to which
at times I'm privy, he surprises me,
talking with a toy mouse in his mouth.
Sauntering down the hallway with it,
he utters sounds with a different tongue.
He drops it and meows at it, urging
it to speak. It can't or won't on its own.
So he picks up the mouthful of mouse again,
lending it his substitute speech,
to find a place where maybe it can.

Wishful Watching

From the floor, he watches me strip the sheets off the bed
and follows to the hall where I put them in the washer
and turn a dial. In the kitchen, I captivate him,
washing our dirty dishes and cleaning up the table.

He'll never thread a belt or read a novel, and yet,
as he watches me intently do these things, I wonder
if he admires that I can or regrets that he's unable.

The world is marvelous to me as well, I tell him,
full of goings-on and doings we might wish for,
though happenstance or need insure we can't or won't or don't.
But to be present and to see such feats, my buddy-pet!

You have talents, too, that I've observed and envy,
so don't begrudge yourself. That others do intriguing things
is worth watching, I agree. Admire all you want but don't regret.

Prescriptions

Irony hits home here
close to the heart:
The cat and I share
the same medicine.

The vet thinks one eye
doesn't see. High blood
pressure can affect
vision. As for me . . .

So in the mornings
we take our medicine
together. Amlodipine.
Still, I'm convinced
it's just coincidence.

Know what I mean?

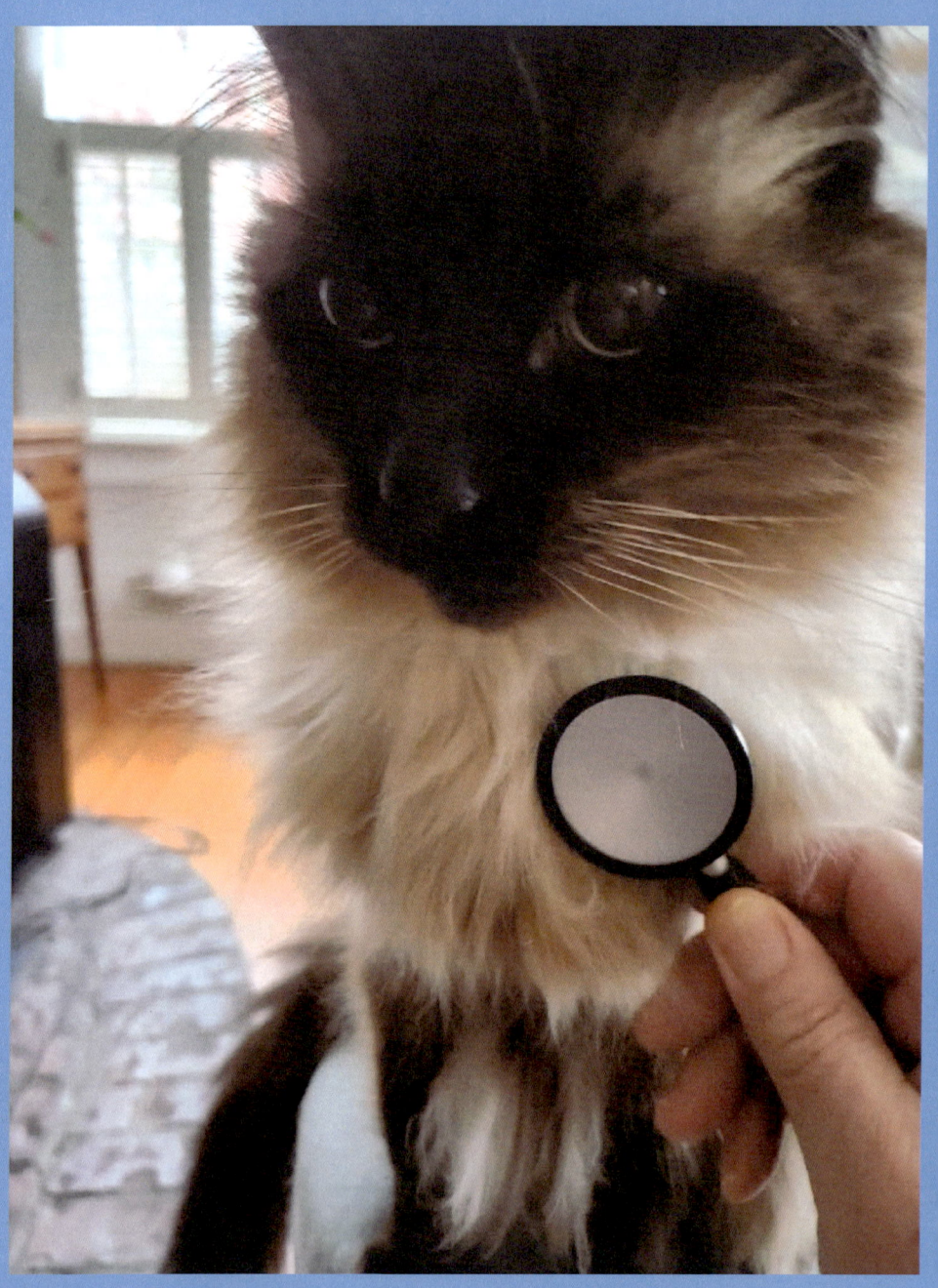

Heartthrobs

The cat sits there comfortably
while I hold the stethoscope
against his chest under the chin.
Then I hear them, huffles of hope
like bubbles bursting under the skin,
or sounds of schoolkids jumping rope,
thumping the pavement again and again.

I hold the silver disc for a minute,
counting the rapid beats, one by one.
It reminds me of a safety head count
of rambunctious kindergarten
children racing out an open
door, like in the story the teacher read
where everything was possible, she said.

When-You-Just-Want-to-Clear-Your-Head-Not-Think Yoga

Bed your weary head.

Drain all mewsings from your brain.

Hang limbs akimbo.

Dream Buddies

The old man and the old cat sleep in bed
like puzzle pieces, birds hunched together
on a winter branch, like peanut butter
and jelly and cheese and macaroni.
When the man turns on his side, then the cat
curls in the concave bay of his body
like a boat at anchor, a crescent moon.

If sleep is the best meditation, then
man and cat meditate like midnight monks,
swamis in nirvana. Their dreams tangle
like mating snakes and spiraling tendrils.
And when the cat wakes from his breakfast dream,
one of his favorite dreams (and the man's too),
they teamwork to make this dream come true.

Watching Cat TV

He likes live action the most.

And nature scenes with birds and squirrels.

If they're snatching seeds, that's always a plus.

When I narrate what's going on,

he's keen to listen but keeps his eyes fixed.

He questions disappearing acts,

but relishes sly entrances.

He tries to catch those wily mice

and has stabbed the screen with his paw

and looked behind it to see where they go.

He can't resist the invitation

to jump in, tail swishing,

to add a few chirps to the script,

but I have to calmly restrain

his die-hard enthusiasm.

Most of the time, though, like you and me,

he watches something playing out

in the natural world, and it fascinates.

Spellbound, he wants to binge

Inspector #1

Determined to get to the bottom of things,
the cat tests gravity by knocking off
a spoon from the table, watching it bounce
on the floor, then jumping down to paw it.
Once it passes inspection, he moves on.
But so much begs for attention, he can't
restore the order he is tasked to probe.

One of my new shirts had in its pocket
a little slip of printed paper,
saying it had been inspected by #1.
Watching the cat reminds me of that,
how one is reassured by a little proof,
repeating a simple test, giving a poke—
deciding what needs disemboweling.

Still, when you get down to the nitty-gritty,
admit cardboard is just cardboard, Kitty.

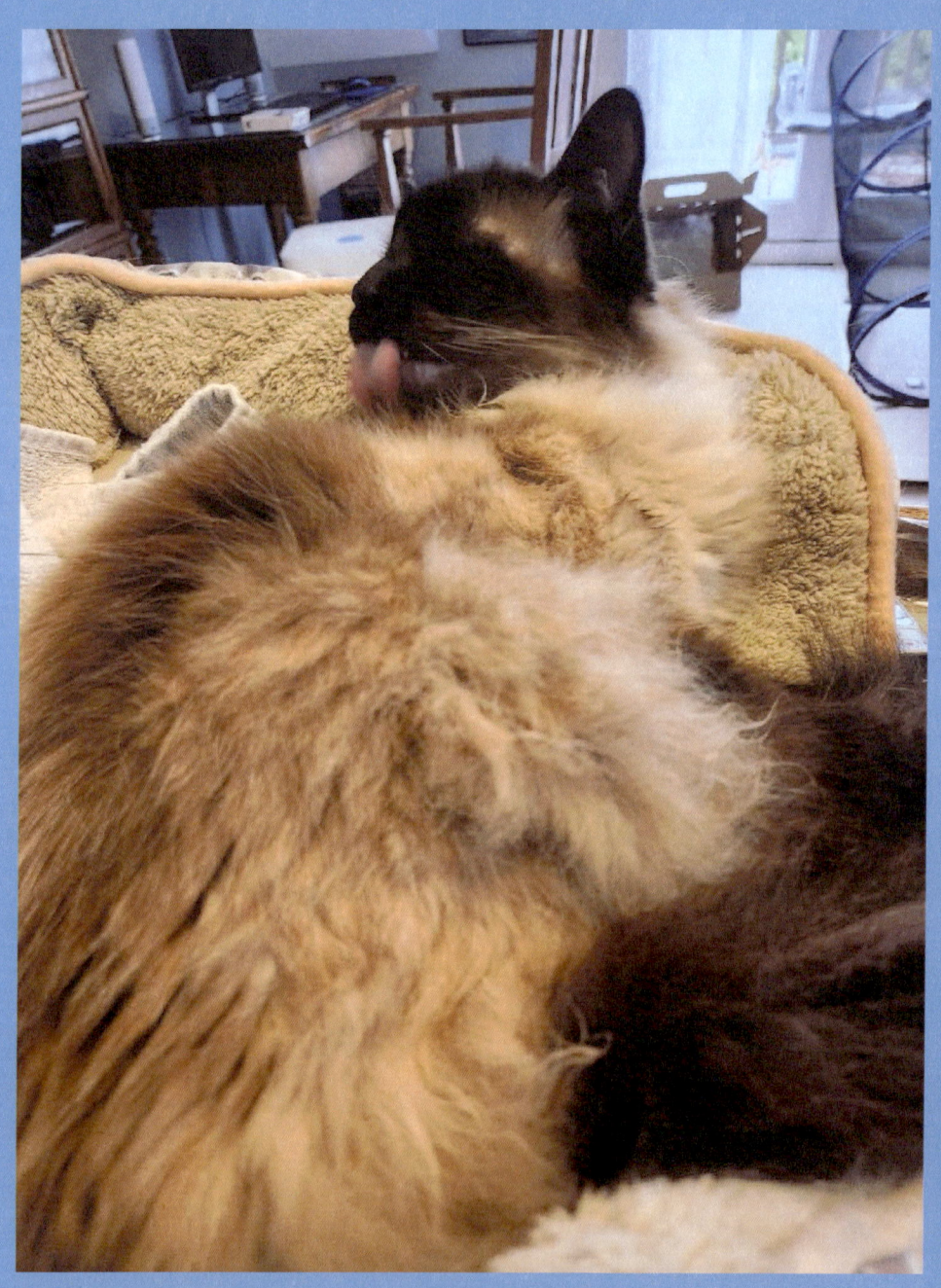

Hair Day

It's a burden he carries, a big job
he's been entrusted with since weaning mom,
a major obligation of his life:
keeping his fur coat clean and his hair brushed.
It's a duty that requires aplomb.

Compare that to women, constantly
fussing with their hair, sitting before mirrors
with brushes and combs, braiding their locks,
experimenting with style and color,
how it might be modified with scissors.

The cat's never sidetracked like that—
he has an assignment, is on
a mission that needs expertise, often:
what a full-body treatment entails.
He's running a private salon*.

*BTW: *he also does nails.*

Lost Sleep Found

I'm a light sleeper;
I lose sleep all the time.
Raining on the roof
wakes me up. So does
having to pee. The cat
wanting breakfast at 5.
That's a tough daily loss.

Yet the cat finds sleep
everywhere, without effort.
In an Amazon box.
On my lap at the computer.
Stretched out in the sunlight
on our Persian rug,
he even finds a sultan's slumber.

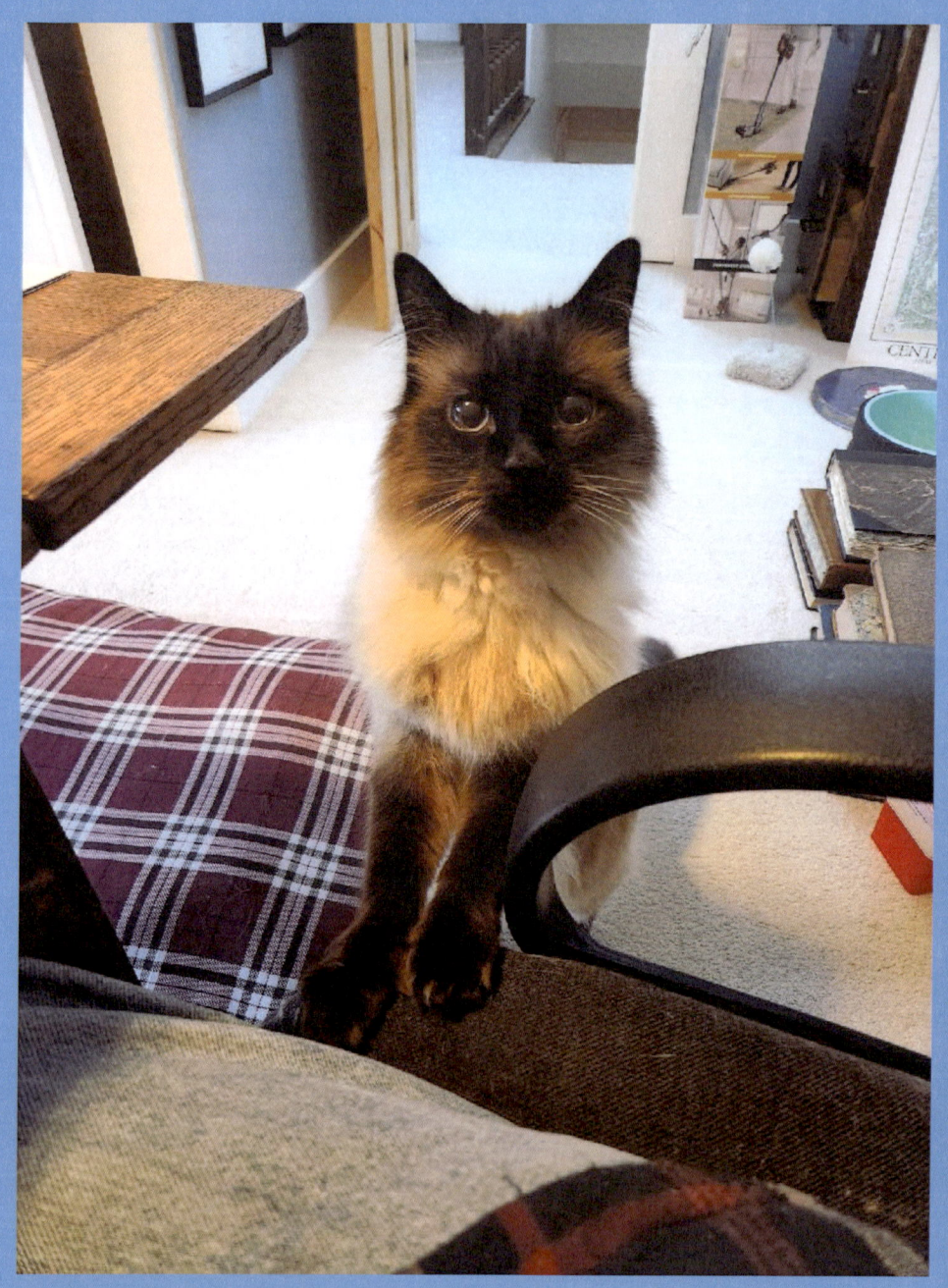

Waiting

Can you wait for what you
want?

At 2 p.m. his wait begins.
4 p.m. is dinner.
If he waits, he wins,
but he's just a beginner.

He rubs my leg
and mutters a meow,
but not to beg,
but ask if now

might be the time
to shorten his wait.
The clock is a hard climb
in his hunger state.

He looks toward the kitchen,
but I'm not in the mood
to move in that direction
and fetch him his food.

If you have a plan
for health and happiness,
stick to it if you can,
Kitty, bear the stress.

He spends the afternoon
sitting, staring, biding
in his cocoon,
in his dreams hiding,

till I give the word
in due time: Dinner!
His rest assured,
he's become a winner.

Was it worth the wait?
The answer is whether
he cleans his plate
and licks his lips together.

Can <u>you</u> wait for what you
want?

On the Porch

I sit on the porch with my companion,
a senior cat doomed to renal failure.
The sun is out and a light breeze blows.
Since he lives indoors, this is a bonus
of smells and sights and sounds. We try
to do this daily, watching the cars pass,
enjoying colors/scents of plants and leaves.

I hold him on my lap like the baby
my son once was, propped up by his senses.
The freshness of the day entrances me
because of the wakeful manner in which
the cat takes what-this-world-can-offer in.
My pacemaker adjusts inner weather
while we bide our time here together.

Pillow Talk

The cat moves to the top of the pillow
to smell my hair and rub his chin in it.
It must be a shampoo that's purr-able.
Ever so gently he takes one of his paws
to reach out and snag my beard, and then
briefly licks a lobe of my ear. He lays
his head down against mine and goes to sleep.

You can read a lot into a gesture
of gentleness from another creature.
That an old cat loves his human buddy?
There's violence in the animal kingdom;
granted, there's desperation to survive.
But how much meanness just to be mean, or
cruelty just to hurt? That's what men are for.

Ramen, the Brahmin

I'd like to think your big black eyes see me
as any other Persian-Siamese
would, without much hoopla and hype,
just another human type
to tolerate, but barely.

Yet it's clear you dote on me too much,
as I on you. We have a mutual crush
as couch potatoes and bed bugs. Our play
capstones each catnap day,
but catnip's needed rarely.

How your black-hole stare snares me
in its gravity! Have I loved you fairly?
I must bear the silence of your knowing
where we're going. Prepare me.

CATalogue

You didn't wash dishes
or empty litter boxes.
Never went shopping
or cleaned up throw up.
You never made a meal
or paid a bill.
Always slept on the job.

Still, you kept yourself clean,
washed your face often.
Only needed one pair of clothes.
Got up early every day,
bright-eyed and bushy-tailed.
Watched me shower
from the toilet seat.
You never missed your meals
and always cleaned your plate.
Purred according to script,
yet could ad-lib as well.
Jumped with joy in play.
Modeled cat fashion
on my desk's laptop.
Cuddled on my tv lap
and nightcapped on my bed.
You always had your eye on me,
but kept your sickness to yourself
like something foreign and feral.

I wanted nothing more nor less than that
you could just continue to be a cat.

Cat at the Window

The cat peeks behind the lace curtain
to get a clearer look through the glass.
For all he knows, he lives in Plato's Cave,
and here's an exit. But surely his life
is real: the tin foil balls, the catnip toy,
the scratching post—all the hideouts
he has found safe haven in. Surely,
they are real. And yet there, beyond the glass,
a breeze stirs, colors sparkle in the sun,
sounds rebound. A different world obtains.

In the summer, the glass becomes a screen,
and then smells are added to the tableau
spread before him. Such mysterious scents!
Now there's even a dark creature flying
across the sky, making a raucous noise.

The cat may never get outside to test
his thesis. What would he make of it all?
Could he have lived a real life there?
He tries to see what he has sacrificed
to let a human being love him here.

Acknowledgments

Grateful appreciation is due the editors of the following magazines where some of the poems and photographs first appeared:

Ink in Thirds: "Reading with the Cat" (with color photograph)

Innisfree Poetry Journal: "Heartthrobs" and "Pillow Talk" (with color photographs)

Last Leaves: "Breakfast *Chez Chat*"

Litbop: Art and Literature in the Groove: "Morning Muse, or, A-musing" (with black-and-white photograph)

New Plains Review: "Adopting a Cat: Checklist" and "Inspector #1" (with color photographs)

Northern New England Review: "Coat", "Scratching Post", "Wishful Watching" (with color photographs)

October Hill Magazine: "Tête-à-Tête"

Poetry Super Highway: "Pacemaker", "Ventriloquist"

The Queens Review: "Dream Buddies"

Route 7 Review: "Lost Sleep Found" and "The Stations" (with color photographs)

Rust and Moth: "Playing with the Cat"

Salt Hills Literary Magazine: "On the Porch"

Shark Reef: "Cat at the Window"

The Vanity Papers: "Prelude (to a Nap), in C Major"

Young Ravens Literary Review: "Bubble Wrap"

VANITY FUR

The **17 hour** SLEEP ROUTINE explained

Full **STYLE**
The Marvelous MRS. **PRADA** + Small Screens, **BIG STARS**

Secrets to getting the best **KISSES** FROM ANYBODY & EVERYBODY

WITH EYES WIDE OPEN BY

RAMEN
THE BRAHMIN

John Delaney retired after 35 years in the Dept. of Rare Books and Special Collections of Princeton University Library, where he was head of manuscripts processing and then, for his last 15 years, curator of historic maps. He has written a number of works on cartography, including *Strait Through: Magellan to Cook and the Pacific*, *First X, Then Y, Now Z: An Introduction to Landmark Thematic Maps*, and *Nova Caesarea: A Cartographic Record of the Garden State, 1666-1888*. These have extensive website versions. He has written poems for most of his life, and, in the 1970s, he attended the Writing Program of Syracuse University, where his mentors were poets W. D. Snodgrass and Philip Booth. No doubt, in subtle ways, they have bookended his approach to poems. His poetic publications include *Waypoints* (2017), a collection of place poems, *Twenty Questions* (2019), a chapbook, *Delicate Arch* (2022), poems and photographs of national parks and monuments, *Galápagos* (2023), a collaborative work of his son Andrew's photographs and his poems, *Nile* (2024), poems and photographs about Egypt, and *Filing Order: Sonnets* (2025). He lives in Port Townsend, WA.

About This Book

Ostensibly about a specific cat, this book has higher hopes—that all cat lovers, and pet owners, will find here some of their own love for these remarkable beings that inherit our homes and our hearts. I have had a life full of dogs and cats, but was always working or going to school, and so I only experienced limited periods of time with my pets. This book shows what happened after I retired, adopted an old cat, and could observe him and fully engage with him around the clock. The time was, as you see, lovingly repaid and cherished. Having sat on my lap or next to me in his desk bed during much of the writing of these poems, Ramen has given them his approval.

If you haven't yet, make room in your heart: adopt a pet.

www.ingramcontent.com/pod-product-compliance
Lightning Source LLC
Chambersburg PA
CBRC102100150426
43198CB00007B/119